MEDICAL MYTHS,
BUSTED!

by Arnold Ringstad

www.12StoryLibrary.com

12-Story Library is an imprint of Peterson Publishing Company and Press Room Editions.

Produced for 12-Story Library by Red Line Editorial

Photographs ©: Odua Images/Shutterstock Images, 1, 9; JPC-PROD/Shutterstock Images, 4, 29; toeytoey/Shutterstock Images, 5; Syda Productions/Shutterstock Images, 6; Louis-Paul St-Onge/ iStockphoto/Thinkstock, 7; Press Illustrating Service/Library of Congress, 8; SomkiatFakmee/ iStockphoto/Thinkstock, 10; CB2/ZOB/WENN.com/Newscom, 11; Fuse/Thinkstock, 12; EM Arts/ Shutterstock Images, 13; sfam_photo/Shutterstock Images, 14; Arman Zhenikeyev/Shutterstock Images, 15, 28; Jerome Delay/AP Images, 16; PeopleImages/iStockphoto, 17; AS400 DB/Corbis, 18, 21; Debora Cartagena/CDC, 19; Peter Wemmert/Shutterstock Images, 20; Henry R. Robinson/Library of Congress, 22; Jason Reed/Ryan McVay/Photodisc/Thinkstock, 23; Olena Zaskochenko/Shutterstock Images, 24; 3445128471/Shutterstock Images, 25; Paul Cooper/Rex Features/AP images, 26; Karin Hildebrand Lau/Shutterstock Images, 27

Library of Congress Cataloging-in-Publication Data
Names: Ringstad, Arnold, author.
Title: Medical myths, busted! / by Arnold Ringstad.
Description: North Mankato, MN : 12-Story Library, [2017] | Series: Science
    myths, busted! | Audience: Grades 4 to 6. | Includes bibliographical
    references and index.
Identifiers: LCCN 2015299452 (print) | LCCN 2016004730 (ebook) | ISBN
    9781632353030 (library bound : alk. paper) | ISBN 9781632353535 (pbk. :
    alk. paper) | ISBN 9781621434689 (hosted ebook)
Subjects: LCSH: Medicine--Miscellanea--Juvenile literature.
Classification: LCC R133.5 .R56 2017 (print) | LCC R133.5 (ebook) | DDC
    610.2--dc23
LC record available at http://lccn.loc.gov/2015299452

Printed in the United States of America
Mankato, MN
May, 2016

Access free, up-to-date content on this topic plus a full digital version of this book. Scan the QR code on page 31 or use your school's login at 12StoryLibrary.com.

Table of Contents

Busted: Vaccines Cause Diseases

Vaccines are medicines that prevent diseases. Scientists have developed vaccines for many diseases. Vaccines have saved millions of lives. If enough people get vaccinated, a disease may go away entirely.

But some people claim that vaccines can cause disease. They say a flu shot can give a person the flu. This is a myth. To understand

why, it is important to know how vaccines work.

The body's immune system protects the body from diseases. The system's white blood cells fight substances called antigens. Often, these are disease-causing viruses. Once the white blood cells encounter the antigens, they create antibodies. These are proteins that help them fight the antigens. When people get sick, their white blood cells destroy the antigens. The white blood cells remember what antibodies to make. Their immune systems can fight off the antigens when they get sick with the same disease.

Vaccines help the immune system defend the body. They contain dead or weakened viruses. This virus is the antigen. But it is not possible for these dead or weakened antigens

> Vaccines help your body build immunity to certain diseases.

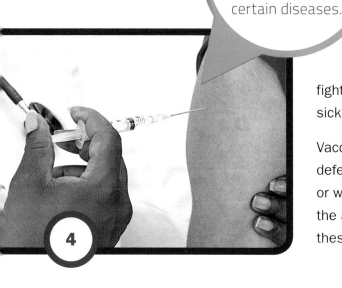

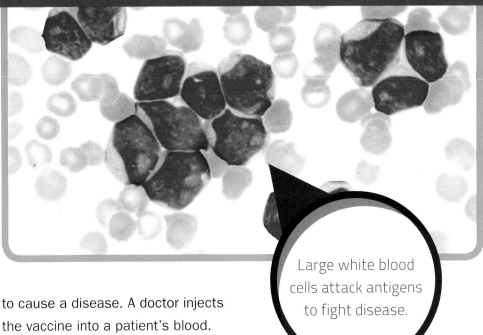

Large white blood cells attack antigens to fight disease.

to cause a disease. A doctor injects the vaccine into a patient's blood. The immune system is able to create antibodies against the antigens. It makes the patient immune to that virus.

Sometimes, a vaccine does not work. A person's immune system may not produce the needed antibody. Later, he or she may catch the disease. But the vaccine itself did not cause the disease.

THINK ABOUT IT

Vaccines have been in the news in the last few years. Some people are convinced vaccines are harmful. Do you agree or disagree? Use evidence from these pages and other sources to support your answer.

179 million

Approximate number of flu vaccine doses that were available in the United States for the 2015–2016 flu season.

- Vaccines are made up of dead or weakened viruses.
- Vaccines allow a person's immune system to prepare to fight a disease.
- Dead or weakened viruses cannot cause diseases.

Busted: Cold Weather Gives You a Cold

Many people believe cold weather causes colds. This disease has the word *cold* right in its name. However, this is a medical myth. Cold temperatures cannot give you a cold.

Viruses cause colds. These microscopic structures enter living things. They make copies of themselves. This causes the living thing to get a disease. A type of virus known as a rhinovirus causes colds.

Viruses can travel from person to person. They spread through the air or through direct contact. When a person with a cold sneezes, viruses fly out in droplets of water. The virus can also spread when people with colds shake hands with others.

Cold weather does not cause colds. But it can make them more likely. People usually stay indoors when it gets cold outside.

Cold weather does not cause the common cold, but it could make getting one more likely.

This puts them in close contact with others. The virus has more chances to spread. Also, cold temperatures make it easier for rhinoviruses to copy themselves. They can infect people more easily.

The common cold spreads through droplets expelled in a sneeze.

10

Approximate number of days it takes to recover from the common cold.

- Cold temperatures do not cause the common cold.
- Rhinoviruses are responsible for giving people the common cold.
- Cold temperatures may indirectly make people more likely to catch colds.

Busted: Radiation Makes You Healthy

In the late 1800s, scientists discovered radiation. This invisible force could make substances glow. It also had many other curious effects. Soon, salespeople took advantage of the public's interest in it. They sold products made with radioactive materials. The salespeople claimed radiation could make people healthy.

By the early 1900s, many radiation researchers were dying of cancer. Among them was the famous Polish-French scientist Marie Curie. People started to understand the dangers

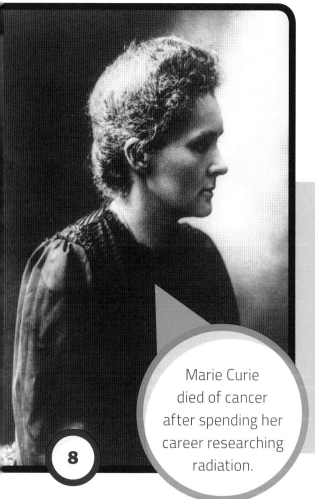

Marie Curie died of cancer after spending her career researching radiation.

MODERN RADIATION TREATMENT

Radiation has uses in modern medicine. Doctors use radiation therapy to fight cancer. The radiation damages cancer cells. However, it can also harm a patient's healthy cells. Doctors plan treatments carefully to reduce the side effects.

of radiation. Yet radioactive products were still sold.

One of these products was radioactive water. In low amounts, it was not harmful. But in high doses, it could be deadly. Businessman Eben Byers drank three bottles of it each day. He died in 1932. He had gotten multiple kinds of cancer.

Companies claimed radiation was natural. They suggested it could increase energy and improve health. Scientists already knew radiation could be harmful. But Byers's death made the danger clear to the public. The US government made stricter rules about medicines. The makers of radioactive products soon went out of business.

1,400

Approximate number of bottles of radioactive water Eben Byers drank.

- When radiation was discovered, people did not understand its dangers.
- Companies released products and medicines with radioactive ingredients.
- The US government eventually banned dangerous radioactive medicines.

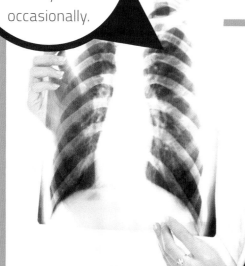

Radiation is a useful medical tool when used wisely and occasionally.

4

Busted: Stopped Hearts Cannot Be Transplanted

Heart transplants have saved many lives. In these surgeries, doctors remove the heart from a patient who has just died. Then, they give it to a patient whose heart is failing. People with transplanted hearts can live for many years. But heart transplant surgeries are challenging. The heart must be moved into the waiting patient right away. If it stops beating, the heart can become damaged. In the past, doctors believed a stopped heart could not be transplanted.

But today, a new technology lets doctors restart stopped hearts. Engineers developed a machine

> Scientists used to think a stopped heart could not be used in a transplant patient.

THINK ABOUT IT

Medical technology is constantly advancing. The research of scientists and engineers helps solve medical problems. What medical conditions do you think scientists will solve in your lifetime? What might these new breakthroughs be?

that keeps a heart alive. The machine pumps fresh blood into the heart. It provides the heart with oxygen and nutrients.

Surgeons in Australia used the machine in 2014. They removed a heart from a dying patient. The heart stopped beating. The surgeons put the heart in the machine. The machine kept the heart alive. When the surgeons were ready for the transplant, they removed the heart from the machine. Then they put the heart into the waiting patient. The heart continued to work and kept the patient alive.

- In the past, heart transplants could not be done with hearts that had stopped beating.
- A machine keeps hearts supplied with fresh blood to keep the heart alive.
- The machine will make more heart transplants successful.

The Organ Care System keeps a heart beating after it is removed from a donor.

Busted: Homeopathy Cures Diseases

Homeopathy is a medical system invented in the 1700s. German doctor Samuel Hahnemann developed it. There are homeopathic cures for all kinds of medical problems. Homeopathy remains popular today. But, there is no evidence that homeopathy actually works.

Homeopathy is based on two theories. The first is the idea of "like cures like." This means a disease can be cured by something that causes its symptoms. For example, onions could cure something that causes teary eyes. The second theory is the law of minimum doses. This idea says the smaller a dose, the more effective it is.

Homeopaths use plants and other natural ingredients to create medicines.

To make doses smaller, homeopathic cures are mixed with water repeatedly. Each time they are mixed, the amount of the original substance gets smaller. The cure goes through the process several times. There is practically none of the original substance left. Homeopathy supporters claim the water contains a memory of the substance it once held. None of the ideas behind homeopathy are supported by science.

Most homeopathic medicines are simply water. They are unlikely to be dangerous. But, using homeopathy in place of treatments that have been proven effective can be dangerous.

$3 billion
Amount Americans spent on homeopathy in 2012.

- Homeopathy was developed in the 1700s.
- Homeopathy is based on two ideas: "like cures like" and the law of minimum doses.
- Modern science does not support the ideas behind homeopathy.

According to the "like cures like" theory, onions could fix watery eyes.

Busted: Humans Use Only 10 Percent of Their Brains

It is common to hear humans use only 10 percent of their brains. Movies and advertising promote this belief. Some products claim to help people use the other 90 percent of their brains. They suggest people can become much smarter. However, brain scientists say this whole idea is a myth.

The myth may have begun in the 1930s. Neurosurgeon Wilder Penfield found parts of the brain that appeared to have no function. He may have thought these areas had the potential to be unlocked. But in reality, the purposes of these sections were later discovered.

The truth is that people use their entire brains. Different parts of the

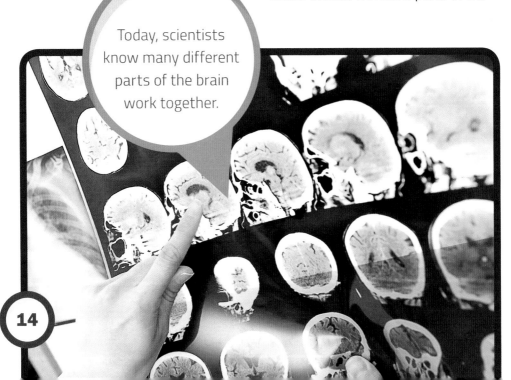

Today, scientists know many different parts of the brain work together.

brain are responsible for different things. People do not use the entire brain all at the same time. Still, many of the brain's parts work together most of the time. The body spends a huge amount of energy keeping the brain running. The brain makes up only 3 percent of a person's weight. Yet it uses 20 percent of the body's total energy.

Movies and TV shows often show people unlocking extra brain power.

3
Weight, in pounds (1.4 kg), of the average human brain.

- Some people claim human beings only use 10 percent of their brains.
- It is suggested that by using more of the brain, people could become much smarter.
- In reality, people use their whole brains, just not all at once.

MYTHS AT THE MOVIES

The myth that humans only use a small amount of potential brainpower is persistent. Movies have been made around this idea. The films *Limitless* (2011) and *Lucy* (2014) both featured this idea. Their characters are able to unlock extra brainpower. They can learn new languages rapidly. They even move objects with their minds. These movies have no scientific basis.

Busted: Ebola Spreads Through the Air

In 2014, a serious disease spread through West Africa. The Ebola virus causes Ebola virus disease. The disease causes severe fever and often death. A few cases of Ebola spread to Europe and the United States. Fear of it spread even faster than Ebola itself. This fear led to many rumors. One rumor claimed the disease was airborne. This would mean it could easily spread through the air. It turned out that this was a myth. To understand why, it is important to know how diseases spread.

The droplets of fluid that fly out of a sick person's sneezes contain viruses. If the droplets are large, they fall to the ground quickly. It is difficult for diseases in large droplets to spread. But small droplets can evaporate and hang

A serious Ebola epidemic struck Liberia in fall 2014.

28,637

Approximate number of people infected in the Ebola outbreak in Africa that began in 2014.

- People created rumors that Ebola could spread easily through the air.
- The ability of a disease to spread through the air depends on the size of the water droplets in an infected person's sneeze.
- Ebola spreads in large droplets, making it difficult to catch through the air.

The Ebola virus is spread through large sneeze droplets.

in the air. It is easy for viruses to spread. Nearby people may catch the disease.

Viruses that move in large droplets can travel at most 6 feet (1.8 m). Then, they hit the ground. They are in the air for under a second. But viruses in small droplets can travel more than 30 feet (9.1 m). They can float through the air for hours. They can infect nearby people.

People worried the Ebola virus spread in small droplets. The rumor was that it spread through the air.

However, it actually spread in large droplets. This made it harder to contain in the air. Most Ebola cases came from people directly touching the bodily fluids of a sick person.

EBOLA SYMPTOMS

Symptoms of Ebola do not appear right away. They start a few days or weeks after infection. Early symptoms include muscle pain, sore throat, and a fever. Eventually, the person suffers from diarrhea, vomiting, and bleeding. If untreated, Ebola is almost always fatal.

Busted: Cigarettes Are Good For You

In the 1940s and 1950s, smoking was extremely popular. Ads for cigarettes filled magazines. The ads suggested cigarettes were safe to use. Some had photos of doctors smoking. Advertisers claimed more doctors smoked the brand being advertised. Others stated their brand of cigarette caused less throat irritation. They said this made it safer. Some ads said cigarettes could boost energy and relieve fatigue. But the benefits and safety of cigarettes are medical myths.

In reality, smoking is the top cause of lung cancer. Scientists estimate 9 in 10 lung cancers are caused by smoking. The ingredients in tobacco smoke reveal why. The smoke can contain more than 7,000 chemicals. Approximately 70 of them have been shown to cause cancer.

The truth about cigarettes was already emerging in the early 1900s. The connection between smoking

LUCKY STRIKE
"IT'S TOASTED"
CIGARETTES

Amelia M. Earhart, first woman to fly the Atlantic by aeroplane

says—

"Lucky Strikes were the cigarettes carried on the 'Friendsh[ip]' when she crossed the Atlantic. They were smoked c[on]tinuously from Trepassey to Wales. I think nothing helped so much to lessen the strain for all of us."

"It's toasted"

No Throat Irritation-No Cough.

This cigarette ad featured famous pilot Amelia Earhart.

SURGEON GENERAL'S WARNING: Smoking Causes Lung Cancer, Heart Disease, Emphysema, And May Complicate Pregnancy.

Today, packs of cigarettes must include a health warning.

30

Approximate number of times more likely it is for a smoker to get lung cancer compared with a nonsmoker.

and lung cancer became well known in 1952. That year, *Reader's Digest* magazine published an article about the dangers of tobacco use. In the 1960s, the US government issued a report with even more evidence. Soon, the government required tobacco companies to put warning labels on their products. It became illegal to claim health benefits from these dangerous products.

- In the early and mid-1900s, tobacco companies claimed their products had health benefits.
- In the 1950s, scientific research showed a strong link between smoking and lung cancer.
- Laws were passed to prevent false health claims from being advertised for smoking.

Busted: "Bad Air" Causes Diseases

Medieval doctors and scientists poorly understood the causes of disease. Doctors invented theories to explain sickness. One of the major ideas was miasma theory. This was the idea that so-called bad air caused disease.

Medieval doctors identified several sources of this bad air. Rotting plants and animals were one source. Marshes and bogs were another. Some even thought earthquakes released poisonous gases from underground. Doctors blamed the bad air for the Black Death. This deadly disease spread through Europe in the mid-1300s. Doctors believed burning certain fragrances could stop the spread of bad air.

Medieval doctors believed marshes caused bad air.

25 million

Approximate number of people who died of the Black Death in Europe.

- Medieval doctors blamed foul-smelling air for disease outbreaks.
- The invention of microscopes allowed scientists to see the microorganisms that cause disease.
- Scientists developed the germ theory of disease to explain the spread of illness.

Belief in miasma theory continued well into the 1800s. People used it to explain the spread of tuberculosis and cholera. These two diseases were common killers. But during this time, scientists began to learn the true cause of disease. They used microscopes to peer into the tiny world of microorganisms. Scientists realized tiny creatures, called germs, spread disease. Bad air did not. Scientists Louis Pasteur, Joseph Lister, and Robert Koch made important contributions to this research. Eventually, germ theory replaced miasma theory as the source of disease.

THE SUCCESS OF GERM THEORY

Joseph Lister was a British surgeon. He helped put the idea of germ theory into practice. He noticed many of his patients got infections after surgery. Lister reasoned that disease-causing bacteria had entered their bodies during surgery. He started taking new steps to keep wounds and his tools clean. The rate of surgical deaths he recorded dropped from 45 percent to 15 percent.

10

Busted: Measuring the Skull Can Explain Personality

In the 1700s, people knew little about how the brain worked. In 1796, German doctor Franz Joseph Gall introduced a new theory. Gall said the brain was divided into separate areas. Each area was connected to a personality trait.

Gall also claimed the brain worked like a muscle. The more a part was used, the bigger it grew. Parts that were used less would shrink. A person's skull would expand to fit growing parts of the brain. This meant the bumps in a skull could be used to understand a person's personality. Gall's theory became known as phrenology. It became popular in the 1800s. Doctors set up clinics where people could have their skulls examined. Inventors made machines to measure bumps on the skull.

As it turned out, a few small parts of Gall's theory were accurate. It is true the brain is separated into different parts. It is also correct that these parts have different functions. But everything else about phrenology is a medical myth. Parts of the brain

A phrenologist studies the skull to determine his patient's political leanings.

do not grow or shrink depending on how much they are used. In addition, the skull cannot bulge out to fit the brain. Instead, a person's brain changes to fit the shape of his or her skull. By the 1840s, most scientists had dismissed the ideas behind phrenology.

Phrenology broke the brain up into different regions based on personality traits.

27

Number of brain areas, according to Gall's original theory.

- Franz Joseph Gall introduced phrenology, the theory that parts of the brain match personality traits.
- Phrenologists believed measuring a person's skull could explain his or her personality.
- Modern science has debunked the ideas behind phrenology.

SCIENCE AND RACISM

In the 1800s, some people used phrenology to justify racism. In the United States, slave owners used it to justify slavery. Slave owner Charles Caldwell claimed African-American slaves had traits making them suitable for slavery. This was one of many cases in which people used incorrect science for racist purposes.

Busted: People Lose the Most Heat Through Their Heads

Many people believe they lose most of their body heat through their heads. They say it is especially important to wear a hat in winter. Hats stop heat from escaping. This idea is actually a medical myth.

The head actually loses approximately as much heat as the rest of the body loses. However, the head and upper body are more sensitive to temperature changes. It feels as though more heat is being lost there. But this is only an illusion.

So how did this myth get started? It likely comes from experiments the US Army did in the 1950s. Soldiers put on heavy winter clothing. But they did not put on hats. They sat

The myth that your head loses the most heat is decades old.

outside in the cold. The experimenters measured heat loss. They observed most heat was escaping from the head. But this was simply because the rest of the body was covered. The misunderstanding of this study may have led to the myth. But the head loses as much heat as the rest of the body loses.

THINK ABOUT IT

The US Army experiment did not require soldiers to wear hats. This caused inaccurate results. How can scientists make sure their experiments are accurate?

Keeping all skin covered in the cold helps keep heat inside.

98.6

Average human body temperature in degrees Fahrenheit (37°C).

- A common myth says people lose most of their body heat through the head.
- In reality, the head does not lose significantly more heat than the rest of the body loses.
- The myth may have come from US Army experiments on body temperature in the 1950s.

25

Busted: Blindness Has No Cure

For thousands of years, there has been no cure for blindness. But that changed in 2013. Engineers introduced a new system that allows blind people to see. The device is known as the Argus II.

The Argus II has three parts. An implant sits inside the patient's eye near the retina. The patient wears a pair of glasses with a video camera. Finally, the patient attaches a small computer to a belt.

Raymond Flynn was the first patient to use Argus II.

The surgery to install the Argus II system takes approximately two hours. The video camera sends images to the computer. The computer processes the images. Then, it sends them to the implant. The implant stimulates the patient's retina. Vision information travels to the brain. The brain interprets the information.

Patients with the system can see differences between light and dark. They may be able to tell whether a person or object is in front of them. Some can recognize extremely large letters or words. This is far from the crystal-clear vision of a healthy eye. But for a person who was previously blind, these abilities represent a huge breakthrough.

Without Argus II, blind people read using Braille.

$100 thousand
Estimated cost of the Argus II system.

- Argus II, a medical system introduced in 2013, can provide blind people with limited vision.
- The system includes an eye implant, a pair of glasses with a camera, and a computer worn on a belt.
- People with the Argus II can distinguish light and dark areas and tell whether objects are in front of them.

Fact Sheet

- Many medical myths come from mistaken theories of the past. Phrenology, homeopathy, and the miasma theory all fall into this category. Scientific advances led to new theories that overtook these old ways of thinking.

- Some medical myths originate in advertising. The salespeople who introduced dangerous radioactive products in the early 1900s that they claimed could keep people healthy created one example of this. The tobacco industry's ads in the 1940s and 1950s represent another case of a myth in advertising.

- Medical myths can come from common sayings or beliefs that spread around despite lack of scientific proof. The beliefs that cold weather can give you a cold, that we use only 10 percent of our brains, and that we lose most of our heat through our heads are all examples.

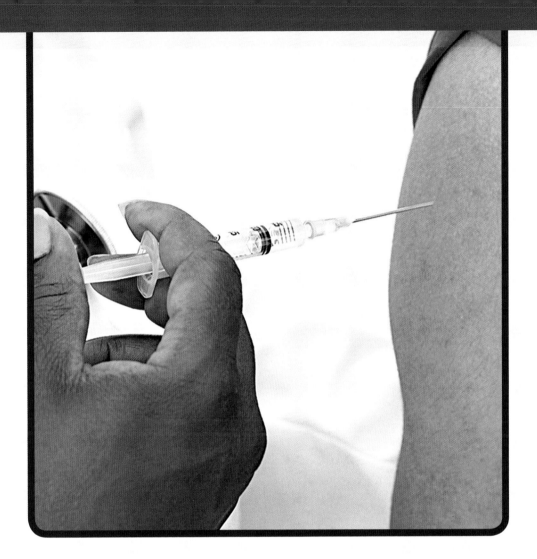

- When medical topics are in the news, myths often arise. The myth that vaccines can cause diseases and the idea that Ebola can spread through the air both became popular when vaccines and Ebola were major news stories. People continue to believe these myths.

- Scientific breakthroughs can turn old ideas into myths. The idea that stopped hearts cannot be transplanted was proven wrong when engineers created a machine to preserve hearts. And the idea that blindness was incurable was countered by the introduction of the Argus II system.

Glossary

antigen
A substance that causes the immune system to react.

fatigue
Tiredness from stress or hard work.

immune system
The organs and systems that fight infections in the body.

implant
Something set securely and deeply in the body.

microorganisms
Creatures that are visible only under a microscope.

microscopic
Only able to be seen through a microscope.

neurosurgeon
A physician who specializes in treatments of the nervous system.

phrenology
The theory that personality can be understood by measuring the skull.

proteins
Substances that are essential for maintaining life.

radiation
Energy that travels through the air invisibly and can damage living tissue.

retina
The part of the eye that is sensitive to light and that sends signals to the brain.

For More Information

Books

Beccia, Carlyn. *I Feel Better with a Frog in My Throat: History's Strangest Cures*. Boston, MA: Houghton Mifflin Books for Children, 2010.

Newman, Patricia. *Ebola: Fears and Facts*. Minneapolis, MN: Millbrook Press, 2016.

Walker, Richard. *Human Body: A Visual Encyclopedia*. New York: DK Publishing, 2012.

Visit 12StoryLibrary.com

Scan the code or use your school's login at **12StoryLibrary.com** for recent updates about this topic and a full digital version of this book. Enjoy free access to:

- Digital ebook
- Breaking news updates
- Live content feeds
- Videos, interactive maps, and graphics
- Additional web resources

Note to educators: Visit 12StoryLibrary.com/register to sign up for free premium website access. Enjoy live content plus a full digital version of every 12-Story Library book you own for every student at your school.

Index

About the Author
Arnold Ringstad has written more than 30 books for students. He likes to read about the history of medicine. He lives in Minnesota.